Magical Dance

By Sally Cowan

I go to dance class each week
with my friends.
We learn different dances
with a range of steps.

There is plenty of space to dance
in our hall.

Jace can spin at a fast pace!

He places two hands up.
One leg is rigid,
and the other is lifted.

Sage has learned hip-hop dance since the age of five.
She can lunge and slide.

At dance class,
we begin with a tap dance.

Our tap shoes make a
click-clack sound.

Then we change to a jazz dance!

Brigit sits while she dances.
She dances with grace.

Dance is great for your fitness and your mood.

Your pulse races,
and your face smiles!

At the end of dance class,
we extend our hands to our toes.

Sam can hold on to all ten digits.

I even dance on stage!

I put on a fancy outfit.

It is nice when all the people clap!

Once, my class went to the city
to see a dance called Swan Lake.

Swan Lake is a tragic tale
about a princess
who turns into a swan!

The dresses had beautiful lace.

We all thought it was magical!

I love my dance class.

You should try to dance
if you get the chance!

CHECKING FOR MEANING

1. What are three kinds of dances? *(Literal)*
2. At what age did Sage start dancing? *(Literal)*
3. Why do the kids do stretches after dance class? *(Inferential)*
4. Which kind of dance do you think would be the hardest to do? Why? *(Evaluative)*

EXTENDING VOCABULARY

pace	What sound does the letter *c* make in the word *pace*? What other words in the book have a *c* with the same sound? What is another word the author could have used instead of *pace*?
tragic	What does it mean if something is tragic? What is the opposite of tragic?
magical	What sound does the letter *g* make in the word *magical*? What other sound can the letter *g* make? What does it mean if something is described as magical?

MOVING BEYOND THE TEXT

1. A hall is a large space to gather, perform and meet. What other events or activities might a hall be used for?

2. You don't need a hall to dance. Where else could you dance?

3. Many dancers begin from a young age, like Sage. Why do you think it helps to start dancing at a young age?

4. Dancers sometimes wear costumes, such as dresses with fancy lace or stretchy tights. Why do you think dancers wear costumes rather than casual clothes when performing on stage?

TIME TO WRITE

Write about which type of dance you would like to try and what you would wear. Explain your reasons.